WRONGFULLY CONVICTED

TAKARA M. JAMES

Edited by

WRITLUXE WRITING FIRM, LLC

Illustrated by

TEMPERTANTRUM TINA

Writluxe Writing Firm
Crime Fiction Publishing

CONTENTS

ALSO BY

Want to read more? Check out these books ...

Desire Boxset

Saving Takara

Shit Black Folk's Don't Talk About

LIT Box Set

Coffee with my Soulmate

Femininity

Chamber Heist

Join my Email List

Scan Me

For information regarding special discounts for bulk purchases, please contact Writluxe Writing Firm, LLC at 615-249-8791.

Interior Formatting- Takara M. James

Editor - Takara M. James

Publisher
Writluxe Writing Firm, LLC
Takara M. James
5987 Lebanon Rd. Ste 402
Murfreesboro, Tennessee 37130
www.writluxe.org

E-BOOK ISBN: 978-1-7359701-1-0
PRINT ISBN: 978-1-7359701-4-1
Manufactured in the United States of America

To all of the African American lives that have been taken away due to police brutality, social and economical injustice, and death as a whole. I love you. And pray your families find justice!

ACKNOWLEDGMENTS

You, the reader, are the reason I've invested in writing this book. Because of you, I felt compelled to write a story that is going to impact so many of our lives. It is my hope that through research, foot work, and dedication, we will continue to fight for ourselves, our families, and our black men and women. Continue to lift your voices, naming those who can no longer speak for themselves. We need change and the only way we will see it is through action. Let's take back what is rightfully ours!

PREFACE

2020, as we all know, has been one of the most challenging years we have faced. From January, losing Kobe Bryant his daughter and the other members of that accident, all through COVID-19, we have taken loss after loss. Many of us have lost loved ones, abruptly, as a result. Importantly, we have also lost many lives due to police brutality.

In the first eight months of the year, over 164 black people have been killed by police. While many of these lives have gone unreported widespread, we have heard these names and mourned their deaths more than ever before. We have cried, seen death on live stream, tried to work, battled job loss, suffered due to lack of resources and so much more.

The purpose of this story is not to simply re-tell the story of how many people have died. It is not even to express that BLACK LIVES DO MATTER, but it is to highlight one of the most important societal issues today, MEN NEED PROTECTION. I think that we have become so focused on how they were created to protect us, that we lack the true understanding that even the protector, needs protection. So, in this story, while you read through some of the most impacting cases that have taken place in 2020, remember, this young man is your brother, he's your son, he's your spouse... and he too... NEEDS PROTECTION!

WRONGFULLY CONVICTED

TO WHOM MUCH IS GIVEN...

> "Love takes off the masks that we fear we cannot live without and know we cannot live within." – James Baldwin

March 2020 was the month that changed life forever. Citizens of Austin, Texas received the COVID-19 mask mandate, along with the rest of the country, and were officially encouraged to quarantine. The coronavirus was unlike anything the world had truly seen up close. This was nothing like the flu or pneumonia. It was taking people out left and right, with little to no warning, and while everyone was frantic and concerned, many people struggled with being forced to social distance and wear face masks on a regular basis. The world thought their only terror was having to protect themselves from the virus, but the black community were being faced with something much more tragic... present-day racism, more than what they'd truly witnessed in a while.

"AYE, Man. Why yo ass over here reading library books and shit. Who comes to the court on that shit? Get out here with the rest of these niggas and hoop."

"Ahmad, bro, first off, you know I don't like that word. Refer to these guys as Kings or by their name. It's enough racial shit going on as we speak so uplift your brother or don't address them at all." Korbin replied.

"Bro, this is exactly why I don't like talking to yo ass. Always on some "higher power" or "politically correct" type shit. Plus, I can barely hear you through that mask anyway!"

"Mahd, you know me, bro. Now if you don't mind, I gotta finish up this read. I'm trying to get this Cyber Security position working with the government. This shit is going to change the game for me bro, I can see me and moms now, hightailing it out this neighborhood into something much better." Korbin said, wishful thinking.

"Aye man, I hate to rain on that pretty boy ass parade of yours, but niggas like us don't make it out. We get stuck here. Me and you done grew up in these streets and now we are in our thirties and still here. There is no exit plan my boy."

"Listen, we all got an opportunity to get out, we just gotta find what works. That said, I'm studying bro, I'll catch up with you." Korbin said, focusing back on his Cybersecurity workbook.

I'M KORBIN DEWAYNE KING, a thirty-year-old, black man who has grown up in the urban streets of Austin Texas. I graduated high school at the top of his class of four-hundred students. As a matter of fact, I graduated in the top-ten percentile and was told that I was "most likely to be successful." After enrolling at The University of Texas at Austin and majoring in Information Technology, I began focusing on the career that could turn all my misfortunes into blessings. I'd spent most of my life trying to grow into a man without the direction of my father. His dad had never been in his life and for all he knew, he wouldn't be able to recognize the man if he saw him.

He figured college and a good job would set the stage for a better life, so he aimed toward that more than anything. He had gotten accepted into college on a full scholarship. Some of the church members of Tabernacle East had come together and written him a check of five-hundred-dollars, to help him get some of the necessities needed for school. Pastor Richards handed Korbin the check, as the congregation cheered in the distance. The echo of praise surrounded the sanctuary and Korbin gracefully accepted with a face full of tears. He was truly grateful for it all, which is why he focused on doing the right thing and excelling to give back.

When Korbin's grandmother, Rosie Lee King, passed away two years ago, he and his mother took over her home and tried to make it the best living space they could. The house was old and barely standing. The windows were drafty, causing winters to be brutal. When storms came during hurricane season, it would always leave light damage behind. Horrible winds and heavy rains caused the old house to have more wear and tear than Korbin remembered as a kid. Nana's house meant a lot to his mother, but I wanted her to have better.

My mom, Carletta King did the best she could with me. She sacrificed sleep, time, and even her sanity most days. She never wanted me to see her struggling, but I was too smart to not see what was written on her face. So, I vowed to maintain Nana's house as best as he could. I knew my mom was getting older. She was now forty-seven, working two jobs, and barely had time for herself. When the pandemic hit, things took a turn, and she was now trying to make ends meet as best she could. Layoffs had been horrible and unemployment claims were hardly being processed. My mom didn't have a home computer, so working from home or at least seeking the opportunities were challenging. That's why I needed this job with the local police department.

After interning at the local police station, during my undergraduate studies, learning the ropes on IT roles, and helping out, I learned about the Cyber Security position and decided to apply. The only problem was, I didn't qualify. I needed at least 120 hours of master's degree credits to even apply for the position, and the role I currently was in, didn't suffice financially. I had transitioned into a field officer position and did lots of desk work since my return but studying for the Cyber exam was priority. With my current IT experience, I could take the certification course to get an entry-level position on the team, while determining if going back for a master's would be ideal for me.

"Yo, aye, y'all check this out. Look at this shit man." One of the guys on the court said. Everyone began to gather around and look at the breaking news report on the guy's phone. "Jonathan Price, killed by Wolfe City officer. Another black man killed by the police," the reporter said.

"What the fuck man?" One of the guys yelled.

I noticed everyone gathered and got up from the park bench. "Yo, what's going on? Why y'all stop playing?"

"Another black man dead." One of the guys said. The basketball court grew silent.

"I'm tired of this shit. It ain't no justice for us. Nobody protects the black man." Someone yelled out.

"Yea, because to them, we just niggas. To them, we don't have an identity, we don't mean shit. We automatically fit the description. We are always guilty of the crime. We don't have knowledge or understanding of the system, so they finessed that shit how they choose. And until we start uniting as a race, we gone always be the underdogs," Korbin said, furious at the breaking news.

"You right bro," some of the guys said.

"You damn right I'm right. We gotta get protected out here or we will be the next Jonathan Price. We already are. No matter how much good we do in this world, as long as we look like this," he said pointing at himself and his skin, "the more they will hate us. They will continue to hate us and spread that same hate until they can't anymore."

"Damn, King, you preaching. Real shit bro," Ahmad said.

"I'm just speaking facts. We have lost Sandra Bland, Breonna Taylor, Jacob Blake, George Floyd, Rayshard Brooks, and countless others. How much more can we take as a race? How many of us gotta die in this wicked ass system before some type of justice is given? They out here killing us. They killing people that look just like everybody I just named. Man or woman, they don't give a damn, so we gotta take a stand. Not to mention the country being run by a racist ass president. I mean, he's openly racist. He's giving white people ammunition to be open with their shit too. Since Trump got in office, shit has been crazier than ever before. These white folks have felt empowered to be openly racist bigots, who are aiming for nothing but our melanated skin. Think about it, the seventeen-year-old white guy, in Kenosha, Wisconsin, who shot at protestors. I mean he openly fucking shot at protestors and then ran toward the cops and they didn't blow his ass off. Ain't no more sweeping that shit under the rug. Fellas, we gotta look out for one another, protect the women and children in this neighborhood." Korbin charged the basketball across the court in anger. Only the whistling of the day's air could be heard in that moment.

In the distance, the Capitol building, and capitol bridge could be seen. As I stepped down from my invisible podium and looked toward the capitol, tension in my shoulders began to rise. The city capitol building was always a reminder of the division between rich and poor in Austin. While I had a job and desired nothing more than to make a difference for my community, I still lived in poverty. With the weight of the pandemic on my shoulders and my mom worrying about how we would maintain Nana's home, I knew I had to do something to make ends meet. Yet, it was hard. Seeing so much death displayed on the news, on the job, and the sadness in the faces of the people of his community, it was too much to carry for someone who was so driven and passionate about saving the world, protecting my family, and building his community, brick-by-brick. As far as I could see, Capitol Hill was just another reminder that no matter how much love, compassion, and effort you poured into the world around you, there will always be a reminder that you are different or that you don't belong.

WHO ARE YOU FIGHTING FOR?

> "Not everything that is faced can be changed; but nothing can be changed until it is faced." – James Baldwin

5th Precinct
Austin, Texas

I made it to work the next morning with a heavy heart. The discussion I had with everyone in the park the day before seemed to put things into perspective for him. Me and all the other black people were fighting a system that was never designed for them. Reflecting back, I remembered times where I was with someone who was racially profiled or had just been harassed, simply because of their skin, but in today's events, things were different. Black people are purposely being targeted and killed and for many reasons, even the oppressors don't know.

"Good morning King, let's have a chat in my office shall we," Captain Grisham said firmly. We walked over to the captain's office, and right before I was ready to sit, the captain said, "shut the door will ya."

"Good morning Cap, what's going on?"

"I hear you're trying to go for the Cyber Security position. I spent some time looking over your file. Hadn't realized you've been with us a little over two years now. What are your plans?"

"I'd like to apply for the position sir. I recognize there are some additional requirements, but it's nothing I'm not willing to work for. I've done a lot of research and--"

"I understand your background, son, I've also seen your work ethic. I reviewed your file and I see that you are missing the education requirements. What if we allowed you to take on the position, while you complete the coursework?"

"Captain Grisham, that would definitely be amazing. I can assure you I won't let you down sir."

"Well, before we get too excited, let me get the paperwork together. I'll need you to follow up with everyone you've worked under, during your tenure here, and let's see if we can get them to write a letter of recommendation. Now, son, I'll say this only once, keep your nose clean. This is a great opportunity for a boy like you and may not come around this easily again. Understood."

A boy like me, I thought. I stood to my feet. Immediately a wave of anger and confusion came over me. The Captain's words, his use of vernacular was completely out of context. Nonetheless, I extended my hand to the Captains, shook it, and said, "I'll be sure to keep my nose clean... sir."

When I made it to my desk, there was a stack of papers waiting for me. "King, finally you bring your ass in. Lieutenant Carson dropped those papers off for you. Looks like you got your work cut out for you today my boy." Ronald Parks said jokingly.

Ron and I had become pretty close since we both began working in the precinct. Ronald had become part of the Cyber team early on and is the reason I had been eager to join. We were the only black males in the district, and while we didn't have any of the major field roles, Cyber was definitely a step in the right direction. Parks and I had attended UT together and were brought in as interns. We kept it cordial early on, to get our foot in the door, but once everyone had become familiar with us, we didn't mind befriending one another and having each other's back.

"Hey man, I may end up in there with you," I said.

"Oh, for real? How long you got until the transition? I thought you needed more education experience or something?" Parks replied.

"Yea, but Cap is trying to get me in the field while I sort this school shit out. He knows I'm good for it. I've already been studying the books you gave me and I'm enrolling back into UT."

"Damn G, that's what's up. I hate you couldn't join me when I went, but you know I understand more than anything about your nana passing. Times have been hard on all of us with this pandemic, but it's good you're getting back focused. You know just from working in here, these streets aint safe for nobody and it ain't shit out there for us anyway." Just as Parks finished his sentence, Lieutenant Carson stepped into the office area.

The fifth precinct was where everyone wanted to work. Once you walked up the brick steps to enter the building, the huge, American Flag waved in the fall air. The tall glass doors led into the open foyer. The marble floors shined and to the left was the receptionist's desk. The receptionist sat behind a tall glass window that surrounded her entirely. The glass was bullet proof and she'd have to speak through an intercom to communicate with anyone who entered the facility. Every door, entrance, and elevator required a badge. You could not access any part of the building without one. From the foyer area were six elevators facing the forward direction. From there you could be taken from the first, second, third, or fourth floor of the building. Suspects who were brought in sat to the right of the receptionist desk. This is where they were fingerprinted and taken to a private room for processing.

Parks and I were on the fourth floor. This was primarily for

Cyber team members and affiliated. I was only there because I'd interned on this floor and was still working there. Our floor didn't deal with field level work. Mostly computers, technology, and getting into encrypted databases. I was good at getting into phones and retrieving data, so that is why I remained on the fourth floor. Tons of sensitive data were stored on this level so there was a level three clearance required to even badge to that floor. In the room where Parks and I worked, there were double doors that led to a large conference-style room. The doors were accompanied by ceiling-high glass windows made of bulletproof glass. Once inside, the entire area was full of 6ft desks with wooden tabletops and metal legs. Each staff member had a comfortable rolling chair, and the floor space was open and well-organized. In one corner of the room was the tech area with long tables. This is where they kept all of the wires, dismembered phones, and other supplies needed to gather electronic data. There were also Tall bar-style round tables with desktop computers on them for connecting devices and retrieving data.

"Alright, everybody listen up. I hear we have a pretty big case coming up. I'm going to need all hands on deck. Y'all know how we do it up here. This facility does not operate without us doing a major part of solving crimes and that is with electronic data research analysis. My IT specialists, I'll need you all to tap into much of the city's camera systems. We will need access to every camera within a 50 mile radius. We will also need total access to all of the 911 calls made on the night in question. I will provide the particulars as soon as I have them, but I need you all prepared. Cyber team, I need you all to follow any breadcrumbs that have been left behind due to system hacks and encryptions in these phone lines. We know how these criminals operate. Let's get the job done so we can all get home to our families. I'll have word on everything momentarily." Lieutenant Carson said.

"Lieutenant, can I speak to you for a second?" I asked.

"Mr. King, what can I do you for?"

"I met with the Captain and he's considering me for the Cyber position. He wanted me to get a letter of recommendation from you and other staff members I've worked directly with. I was wondering if you'd be able to provide that as soon as possible."

"I'll get right on it son. Glad to hear you are planning to take a step ahead. You've done great work in this office, so I know you'll definitely add to the morale with Cyber."

"I appreciate that sir. I look forward to a continuous work relationship."

Just as they were wrapping up their conversation, Lieutenant Carson got a phone call. He immediately stepped into the common office and called everyone to the briefing room.

"Alright, I know what we previously discussed, but it looks like we will be taking things in a different direction. "Ondre Jamal Johnson, black, male, shot and killed this evening by two police officers," Lt. Carson said, pointing at the image on the Smart Board. "Members of the community say that he was not armed, police staff says that he was, this is outside of our jurisdiction, but we are next in line to cover, since the precinct is directly involved in this case, down at the 4th. I need you all to dig up everything you can find on this guy. Every mugshot, every gun and money photo on his social media, every nappy whore he's been involved with over the years, I need this information on my desk within three hours. We will then need to brief the team downstairs with our findings. Not for a second should we misunderstand that our job is to protect our own first! Now get to work."

I couldn't breathe - I had just been with Ondre less than twenty-four hours ago. I need some air but knew that I was on borrowed time right now. There were no breaks on big cases like this. It was the second one I've seen since I began working at the 5th, and I knew how intense it would get in the office. *Why does this shit keep happening to my people?* I thought. I quickly ran into the restroom, had a silent cry in the stall, and washed my face right after. The facts were, I had known Ondre since we were kids.

Ondre was one of the guys at the park yesterday and in less than twenty-four-hours, Ondre was now dead. *That could have been me*, I kept thinking. I tried to brush those thoughts from his mind, but the reality was, I was a black man, trapped in a system that wasn't designed for me. No matter how much I tried to find ways to escape this reality, this was it, it was proof that life would only continue to get harder, unless change was to follow.

———

BACK IN THE OFFICE, it was now time to dig into this case unlike any other. The team worked swiftly against time, trying to come up with as much evidence as possible to understand the true outcomes of what had happened between Ondre and the police shooting. So far, based on what we'd collected, video showed that Ondre complied, but because he questioned them, and restated his rights, it caused hostility among the officers present. They began to get frustrated and take unethical actions, all displayed in the video content retrieved.

"Can you believe this?" I asked Ronald.

"Look, regardless of how I feel, you know this is definitely no place for this convo. Drop it Kor. This is our job. We took an oath to do just that when he agreed to be here. Don't let these cases trick you out of your position." Ron replied.

Korbin felt trapped. He had so much to say, so much on the heart, but he knew the only safe place was the streets, among those who felt exactly as he did, and he couldn't wait to get off work and share his frustrations.

Lieutenant Carson came back in the common office area. "What have we got?"

Some of the members of the team began sharing the latest details.

"So far Lt., looks like this was an injustice. Johnson did comply, but things got out of hand when he began questioning the officers."

"What makes these people think they can talk back to police officers? How is that supposed to end fairly for anyone?

Not all officers are like that," I said.

"Like what? What are you saying boy?"

"Not all officers are--" Before I could finish the LT. demanded me to his office.

"Look King, I don't know what your shit is today, but I'm not for it! If you have a problem, I suggest you make that known right here and right now! The Lt. demanded. "Better yet, I think you should take the rest of the day off. Clock out, go home, and you think about what side of justice you want to be on, because we have a job to do, a duty, a responsibility to the members of this precinct and if we don't fulfill that, then we are leaving our men open and accessible. Do you understand me? Now, get out of my office."

I made it to my desk, got my things, and headed for the door. Parks looked at me, shaking his head. "Sometimes being the smartest in the room don't benefit you. You'll learn one day," Ron said. I shook my head and walked away. It was the first time I felt like I didn't recognize Ron. How could this be the same person I've been around all these years and he was so willing to sacrifice his beliefs and ethics over the career? I mean of course, working at the precinct afforded a lot of opportunities. Getting stopped, traffic tickets, attending big city events and so much more, especially being my age, it was easy to allow those types of things to entice you, but it all came at a price, one that I was going to have to quickly learn how to balance.

When I made it to the first level of the precinct, I could feel the weightlifting from my shoulders. I'd spent most of the day feeling heavy, feeling as though something important was missing from my life. None of the studying, being the smartest in the room, or even leading the small discussion the other day could compensate for his feeling of being lost in translation. I recognized that it was no longer about money or success, it was now about trying to really survive and make it to the next day. That was all I wanted these days. Not just for myself, but for my friends, those in my neighborhood, and especially for my mom.

I grabbed my cell and dialed my mom's number. "Hey ma, what you got going?"

"Nothing baby, just picking up around the house. How is work?"

"All is good ma, I got off a little early today, wanted to see if you needed anything before I headed to the court?"

"No, baby, I'm good. I'll be making some dinner around 7, so you be sure to be home please."

"Okay, ma, it's only noon now, so that give me time to hoop with the guys and get home and cleaned up. I got work tomorrow anyway, so no plans to be out too long."

Once I got off the phone with mom, I quickly called my best friend Amahd. "Yo, Mahd, y'all at the court?"

"Hell yell, you coming to study again?" Amahd said jokingly.

"Nah, I needed to talk to everybody on the court. Another talk like the other day."

"Aight, bet, I'll let everybody know. You on the way?"

"In route now, see y'all in like 20."

"Bet!"

I ARRIVED at the court and saw everybody hanging around. When I stepped out of his car, I immediately saw Amahd waving for me to come over. A group of people were huddled around my favorite bench, and eager to hear what I had to say. I stepped on the bench and began my speech:

"I don't think this information has reached the public yet and I hate to be the one to share it, but our very own, Ondre Johnson, was killed by police earlier today. The case came across my desk at the precinct, and again, while I shouldn't be sharing this, I later learned that Ondre did nothing wrong. Look, I know we don't fuck with 12 out here, and that's cool. I respect you for even messing with me under the circumstances. I ask that you do not go out and do anything crazy, but I am asking that we begin protesting. I don't give a damn about y'all fear of consequences or none of that shit. We have to end this. We have to take a stand and end brutality among our people. Things are getting completely out of hand and I know that if it was one of you, you would want us all out here fighting hand and fist to get you justice. Ondre was like a brother to many of us, especially me. Whatever we gotta do, we need to do that."

Everyone began shaking their heads and agreeing in unison.

"We need to have a meeting this Saturday. Let's meet at The Underground and discuss how we need to move from here. For those of you with military training, I need a list of names. Any of you who have felonies or the like, I need a list of names. I am going to work to protect you guys and ensure that you are never in compromising positions, but we will RIGHTFULLY protest. We will be peaceful and comply with the law, but I need to make sure we are together on this, more than anything. This is for Jonathan Price, Ondre Johnson, George Floyd, Sandra Bland, Breonna Taylor and so many others who have lost their fucking lives. I appreciate y'all time. Let's meet at The Underground, Saturday around 7."

"You about to bail out?" Mahd asked.

"Yea, moms making dinner and I promised I'd be home for it. Plus, I got more studying to do. Captain said he's going to put in a good word for me."

"You sure that's what you wanna do, man?"

"It's my passion and unless I do it for myself, I gotta get my foot in the door. What better way than this?" Korbin said.

Me and Ahmad shook hands before I walked away from the court.

THE PLAN

> "To be a Negro in this country and to be relatively conscious is to be in a rage almost all the time" – James Baldwin

I had spent the last few days, gathering his thoughts, planning, and really thinking about how things would unfold from here. I understood that there was no straddling the fence. I would have to choose between black and blue, but I never felt I'd have to. I wasn't an officer. There was no need to act as though my life was based on being a police officer, but I knew the rest of the world categorized me. That was the problem with being on both sides of the law. Justice and injustice. Like never before I was part of both classes of individuals and was beginning to see just how wicked the system truly was.

Saturday was only a few days away. Ahmahd had come over a few times to help plan everything, but he was never known for organizing. Not on paper. He was the guy that would always get people in one room, regardless of the type of issues they had. It's why he and I had been friends for so many years. Unlike a lot of guys in the hood, Ahmahd was solid, and no one could change that.

"Korbin Dewayne," mom called from downstairs. I was sleep.. The long shifts and even longer nights had taken up much of my time. I'd promised mom I'd help with some important paperwork she asked for assistance with but had been too busy these last few days.

"Korbin!" She yelled out again, but still nothing. Mom walked up the creaking stairs and to the room where I had slept over the years. The door was made of solid pine. It had been put up a few years ago when the last door that nanny had in the home, began to rot. We were still trying to fix up the old place, but this was the best we could do for the time being.

"Korbin, get your butt up."

"Ma, what's up?" I said wiping my eyes and stretching my arms. I slid up against the wall and pushed the covers back, as if I was getting out of the bed.

"Korbin, don't you have to work today?" His mother asked.

"Yea, but I'm going in a little later. I told the Lieutenant that I would be in late today. I haven't gotten much sleep this week and needed a little more rest. What's up, everything good?"

"Yea, baby, but I needed you to help me with some paperwork remember?"

"Oh, shi-shoot, I forgot ma. I'm sorry, let me get up and get myself together."

"No, you get some rest or whatever you need to do. We can sort through the documents later, but Korbin..." she said, gazing sternly at me, "we really need to get this done as soon as possible."

"What kind of papers ma?"

"Deeds for the house and stuff. I just want to make sure things are organized."

Without second thought, I agreed and got out of bed. I didn't think anything about mom wanting to sort out whatever documents she had because she was always trying to organize or get things done. I had an hour left before needing to be at work, so I got myself together, kissed mom on the way out and headed for the door. It was Friday, one day before the big meet. My whole neighborhood had plans that would change the dynamic of their neighborhood, and the city of Austin for good.

If you look far enough, out of the neighborhood, you could see the state capital and the Congress Capital Bridge. We have always seen it as the divide between the rich and poor. What other reason would there be than to have it split up the city of Austin into two distinct parts. A host of parked cars were lined up along the sidewalks. These neighborhoods didn't have driveways and usually, there was always a parked vehicle accident, when cars would come speeding down the streets of the neighborhood. I took a look around. As I came to a stop at the intersecting streets, Cherry and Dunlap, I looked at all of the flower shops, bakeries, and residential landscapes that had barely survived in his neighborhood, and with the uprising COVID-19 global pandemic, more businesses were closing indefinitely. Cherry & Dunlap were widely known for their mom and pop shops, owned by black men and women who took pride in being successful business owners. My thoughts were interrupted when I heard the car behind me beeping their horn and yelling, "it's a STOP SIGN, not a RED LIGHT!" I quickly sped off, heading for the precinct.

When I arrived, I scanned my badge and walked into the double door entry of the police station. I still struggled to ignore my thoughts as there was so much noise at every turn. The sound of people shifting about in the waiting room, officers walking throughout the area talking, the smell of stale coffee in the air, and handcuffs rattling about, filled the opened space like loud instruments. As I headed for the elevator doors, I was called to the Captain's office.

"Have a seat son."

"Yes sir, Capt."

"There're rumors around here that you're engaged in some

protest against the department. I hear you are familiar with the boy who got killed recently, the open case your team has been working on..." Captain said.

"Which boy? I fear that because there are so many instances of this happening, that I am unclear on which person you're referring to, respectfully."

"Instances of what?"

"Respectfully sir, the various cases of black men being targets for racial injustice, especially the lack of proper police procedural and due justice when being accused of a crime."

"You know what King, my grandfather, God rest his soul, fought hand and fist for this country many years ago. During the fight of the Civil War, he did what was necessary to fight for this country and protect what was left of the peace and integrity the world needed. There will always be a fine line between social activism and policing, son, you will have to choose a side one way or another."

"That's the problem Captain. Either way the coin is flipped, I am a black man in America. The justice system, police procedural, or none of that applies to me as a black man, because there will always be strikes against me. I have worked hard to be here sir. I have studied, gotten the education, done all that was necessary to pass the background checks to get here, on top of having a clean record, but when I step outside of those doors, I'm not looked at as a person with power or the ability to change. They don't care about my passion to serve and protect, instead, I'm labeled by my appearance. I'm labeled by how I dress, talk, walk, everything. You know, Langston Hughes once wrote,

"I, too, Sing America.
I am the darker brother.
They send me to eat in the kitchen
When company comes,
But I laugh,
And eat well,

And grow strong.
Tomorrow,
I'll be at the table
When company comes.
Nobody'll dare
Say to me,
"Eat in the kitchen,"
Then.
Besides,
They'll see how beautiful I am
And be ashamed—
I, too, am America."

This may not make sense to you now Captain, but there is a lot that the world doesn't give my people credit for. It's time for a change. We are battling a virus that no one knows anything about. People are dying more quickly due to COVID than they are by gun violence or the flu. You have mothers and children struggling and without proper resources, because they live in communities that no one gives a damn about. So, while I understand your passion for not wanting to see an officer under your leadership equally protesting in the same community he grew up in, unless you come to these neighborhoods and see what is going on firsthand, I have to honor this badge and continue to serve and protect my people."

"King, I hear your argument, but it is not something that is a good reflection on this department and the other officers, of other ethnicities, who deserve an equal level of respect and protection. That said, I think you should take some time off and get your head clear son. This is serious business that goes on behind these doors. We carry out the oath of this department and for those we continue to fight to protect, but we also have families to go home to at the end of the day. You have done great work here, but I need to know that the brothers and sisters in blue are the ones you are willing to protect, without question or doubt. I'll give you until next Friday to give me your decision. In the meantime, I'd suggest you contact your Union rep as this is something that they handle. We shouldn't have had this conversation without someone present, but you know that I've been supportive and try to look out for you."

I was headed for the door when the Captain asked me for my badge and gun. "Until further notice, you are a civilian. Your badge and gun will be here when you make your final decision."

What I'd just heard was hard to digest, as I understood there was truly a choice to be made between being black or being blue. Yet, there was weight turning in my badge and gun for a few days. It put things into perspective for me and it was the most clarity I'd had in a while. To someone else, it may have appeared to be a forced proposition on their political stance, but to me, I realized the Captain was doing something much bigger than anyone would have expected.

BAD TIMING

> "The paradox of education is precisely this—that as one begins to become conscious one begins to examine the society in which he is being educated." – James Baldwin

After meeting with a few people for Saturday's protest, I headed home for the night. It was a quarter to eight and I knew tomorrow would be a long day, so rest was critical right now. As soon as I made it through the entryway of my home, I could smell my mom's cooking. "Ms. King, I know that aint you throwing down in the kitchen, now is it?" I laughed, but my smirk changed when I saw the serious look on mom's face. She sat at the table, among a pile of papers, ushering for me to come take a seat.

"Ma, what is it, are we behind on the mortgage?"

"Korbin, my son," my mom said, as she rubbed her hand against her my cheek. "I have been holding this from you for far too long now. I pray that you can understand a mothers need to protect her child, no matter how old you get, and that I had no intentions of drawing this out any longer than it already has been. Son, I have stage four cancer. I have known for a little over three months now. I couldn't come to terms with it and still haven't, but it is time that I prepare myself, regardless of the outcomes. You have been studying for your test and have finally began rebuilding your life, so in no way did I want to put this burden on you." My mom reached to grab my hand, but I stormed out of the front door, pulled my hoody over my head, headphones in, and began playing music loudly to drown out my silent cry.

In the distance, I could see the Capital Bridge well lit, from the view of my neighborhood. My anger intensified. This was one of those constant reminders of how horrible life had turned out to be. No matter how far ahead I aimed for, there was always something pulling me back. My passion to change the world was only a glimpse of who I am, but there were so many things keeping me from being the hero I desired to be. Just as I turned the music down, I heard gunshots coming from behind him. I dared not to look back, instead I ran as fast as I could up the block, making a right on Cherry, in front of the old buildings I was staring at earlier that morning. Anybody who grew up in the hood know that if you're naked in the streets, never try to investigate who's shooting. As soon as I made the turn on the corner, police sirens and lights filled the area, and I was surrounded.

"Thank God you all are here. There were shots fired down the block. I'm a fellow officer, the suspect could be getting away."

"Put your hands above your head," one of the officers shouted.

"Listen, I'm a fellow officer, I work for the 5th Precinct. My mom lives down the block and shots were fired, I need you all to get down there and check on the well-being of the folks in my neighborhood."

"I repeat, put your hands above your head," one of the officers shouted again. Frozen in fear, I did just that. As I positioned my hands above my head, I saw Ronald coming from around the corner on foot.

"Captain Grisham was just shot, we need medical treatment immediately," Ron shouted.

"Ron, please explain to these officers that I am an officer also," I said. Ron walked over to the officers who stood with their guns pointing at me. He spoke with one of the leading officers on the scene. "What happened here," Ron asked. "This man was seen running from the same area you said the shooting took place. I'm sure he's the only one in the area who could have likely done this crime," the officer said. "I see. It is quite ironic that this gentleman was released of his badge earlier today. He's part of the activism against officers in this neighborhood," Ron replied. "So, he is an officer," one of the cops asked. "Was... He was an officer. Book him, Ron replied, and headed back to his vehicle."

HEAVY IS THE HEAD THAT WEARS THE CROWN

"The most dangerous creation of any society is the man who has nothing to lose." - James Baldwin

"Korbin King, you have the right to remain silent. Anything you say can and will be used against you in a court of law. You have the right to an attorney. If you cannot— "The words appeared to dissolve in the night's air. I couldn't believe that my tenure as an officer would lead to this moment. If you're curious why a black police officer would run, then you haven't spent much time in the hood. Actually, you haven't spent much time truly understanding what it is like to be black. It doesn't matter who you are as a black person. When shots are fired in the hood, you run. Unfortunately, running led me to this very moment, one that would change life forever.

Interrogation
5th Precinct

"Mr. King, I know that you understand how this works. If you cooperate with me, we can get this thing done, get you processed, and move along with our evening. How does that sound?" Detective Casey and Detective Berlew were both from IAB. They'd been called from Detroit to assist with the case.

"Shouldn't I have my union rep present," I asked?

"That won't be necessary, but if you'd like, we can make the call for you." Detective Casey replied.

"I'd rather do it myself." After a few moments of silence, Lieutenant Carson, my boss, walked into the room with a lawyer.

"Gentlemen, can we have the room?" Lieutenant

Carson asked. After a few stares, both detectives left and gave Carson and the lawyer the room.

"Korbin, I heard about what happened. Your mom is worried about you and wanted to know how you were doing. We haven't had an opportunity to get you a call to her yet, but she was able to call a lawyer for your defense. I'm not sure what has taken place. There have been rumors surrounding this issue, but IAB is all over it. I can't really discuss anything with you, but I at least wanted to bring in your lawyer. His name is—."

"Korbin, I'm Derek Edwards, criminal lawyer and have worked on many Supreme Court cases. I am here to represent you in any capacity you may need. I also have a team of individuals working closely with us regarding your case and ensuring your mother is updated throughout this process. I am—."

"How do you know my mother," I asked? After a brief moment and attorney Edwards asking for a private moment with me, I learned the true identity of who he was. After another moment of silence, I couldn't believe I was sitting across from my father. I couldn't believe that it had taken all of these years to even have a face-to-face with him, and I made sure he knew that.

We went back and forth for a while, and as much as I wanted to argue and yell at him for being absent in my life, I took the high road and let him try to get me out of this.

"Look, Derek... Edwards, whatever you'd like to be called, no disrespect, but I definitely didn't do this. I don't know what happened. I was angry about something my mom shared with me. I went for a walk, heard shots knowing I wasn't armed, and I ran for cover. Look, I live in a bad neighborhood. My badge and gun were taken earlier today, and I honestly didn't want to be the next black man on the news because I was walking while black." I gave him all the information he needed. I didn't want to go down for something I didn't do, and if his reputation was as good as he said, I hope like hell he can get me out of this.

Edwards stepped out of the interrogation room for what seemed like forever. All I could hear were footsteps passing by, people talking, and the sound of the AC unit going in and out. All I could think about was my mother and how I would be missing the protest tomorrow. Somebody needed to speak up for our people, and there is nobody better than me, especially after this. The bigger problem was, I didn't know who got shot. Everything happened so fast, I didn't take a moment to hear who Ron said was shot. For them to take me in or assume that I had something to do with this meant that something big had happened. Edwards walked back into the room and placed his hand on one of the metal chairs.

"Look, son,..." Before he could finish, I glared at him in a way. He quickly adjusted his tie and began speaking again.

"Mr. King, Captain Grisham was the person who was shot. He's in critical condition, and due to the nature of what happened earlier today, you are the primary suspect. At this time, it is hard to pinpoint a timeline of events that could have led to the altercation, along with why your captain was making a personal visit in the first place. That said, you are being released with a court appearance next Thursday." Edwards kept talking, and while I understood everything he was saying, something just wasn't adding up... *why would Cap be at my address that time of night*, I thought to myself? Edwards stopped talking, and the two detectives came back for their final words. I could tell they wanted to pin me for this, but I was an officer of the law as well. Detective Berlew was black. If anyone should have understood what was happening, it should have been him.

I gathered what little I could that wasn't already in evidence and headed for the building's double door exit. Before I could make it out, Edwards came running up behind me. Nervous and on edge, I jumped until I recognized who he was. Once we made it to the parking lot, I couldn't help but cry as a sign of relief. "Look, son, I can't really imagine what this moment must feel like for you, but as a black man who grew up in your same neighborhood, I know this all too well. Some folks don't make it out of the system, yet they find themselves trapped in it too easily. I made a promise to myself and your mother years ago that no matter what she felt, if you ever needed me, I would be here, and I'm going to fight like hell to keep that promise."

He offered me a ride home because mom was in no condition to drive. On the ride to my neighborhood, he shared that someone in the department has it out for me and that this could potentially be a setup. I shared with him that, while Cap and I had our words earlier that day, there had never been bad blood between us, and I'm always respectful of my superiors. I just couldn't understand where the tables were turning and who was doing the pushing. Then I thought back to how Ron handled things at the scene and how he was "all of a sudden" on the scene, moments after everything had taken place. He was also, coincidentally, coming from the same direction I had come from, but I didn't understand why he was coming from there, and the other cops had met me from a different direction. I mentioned all of that to Edwards, before shouting "I have a plan."

UNITED WE STAND

"You were born where you were born and faced the future that you faced because you were Black and for no other reason. The limits of your ambition were, thus, expected to be set forever. You were born into a society which spelled out with brutal clarity, ad in as many ways as possible, that you were a worthless human being. You were not expected to aspire to excellence: you were expected to make peace with mediocrity." - James Baldwin.

Six days ago, I had been faced with some of the most difficult challenges of my life. I thought that my struggles were primarily trying to have better and see better for the sake of my family, but in a single night, I had lost my career, gotten news of my mother being sick, saw my absent father for the first time and was on trial for murder. It all made me reflect on how love is the only thing that drives out hate. If it is love that holds things together, molds even some of the most shattered pieces, then maybe it is love that can help reshape what seems like inevitable, irreconcilable circumstances. That is why today will be a stance in history that no one has ever witnessed. Today is when we, as black people, come off the streets and walk right into the justice system with the most powerful thing that only God has given us, and that is love. With so much hate in the world, one could only rely on spreading what has never been given to us. Today is not just about me fighting for my own rights or justice. It is about fighting for every person who has never made it to this point in their story.

This is for Rayshard Brooks, Daniel Prude, George Floyd, Breonna Taylor, Atatiana Jefferson, Dante Wright, Aura Rosser, Stephon Clark, Botham Jean, Jonathan Price, Philando Castille, Alton Sterling, Freddie Gray, Eric Garner, Ahmaud Arbery, and many others who have lost their lives due to the disregard and fear of police officers. We have spent the entire pandemic struggling to find food, resources, work, and so much more, but our biggest struggle has been trying to fight a system that refuses to let us in. So, instead, we will walk through the front doors of that same system, strapped with more than our tears and our prayers, but our knowledge and power. See, while the world has continued to fight against us, it hasn't recognized that it has only prepared us for this moment. All of the research, investigations, social media protests, and so much more have done one very unexpected thing: unity among our people. Today we stand black with our brown skin sisters and brothers, the Asian community, and all the other races who are sick and tired of the same shit, of seeing the same shit, the hate, the disregard, the deniability, and the lack of justice prevailed in this country. We live in a time where a man can be sentenced to life for killing a dog, but a police officer can go lay next to his wife and kids after killing an unarmed, compliant black man. My mother can't breathe, nor can the mothers of the astronomical number of lives that have been taken at a moment notice, because lying in bed next to your loved one gets you killed, getting candy and a drink from the store gets you killed, walking while black gets you killed, selling cd's gets you killed, simply breathing gets you killed! Today, we fight. Not with riots, not with destroying our own neighborhoods, not with hatred in our hearts, but a fight that can only come from love and compassion.

For the first time, my people made it to Capitol hill. I could see my neighborhood in the distance, and as I looked behind me, climbing the steps to the court entrance, I was proud to see my people standing behind me. The crowd was mixed with all races, black, brown, Asian, Indian, Mexican, Caucasians, all applauding and cheering as this would be a day history would never forget. I was still very nervous, but my mother was to my right, and my lawyer and reunited father were to my left. When Ahmahd learned what happened, he gathered all the people who were supposed to march with us last weekend and had them bring their voices today.

Once we made it into the building, went through security, and entered the courtroom, I recognized some faces that I was very proud to see. Travon Martin's family were seated near the front. Jonathan Price's family were seated near Trayvon's, and so was Ahmaud Arbery's family. I saw a few of Sandra, Philando, and Breonna's family to the left of the room. My heart was full because I couldn't imagine what it took for them to get here and the pain it may have resurfaced. My father had pulled so many strings in such a short time to make this happen. I knew he was likely overcompensating, to some degree, but he had done what he'd promised. This was not the time to be upset about a life I hadn't had with him because I wanted to fix this. Allow both of us to have a future to get to know one another.

The rest of the crowd filled the courtroom to capacity. Despite covid and wearing masks, everyone wanted to be present for what was about to take place. Nine judges were sitting along with a long table with microphones in front of them. Each of them asked questions, challenging the defense. I watched my dad work and articulated himself in a way that assured me I was his son. His intelligence, demeanor, mannerisms, and the like were in full display, and I sat proudly next to him. There were a few moments where minimal evidence was presented, but it was all stuff anyone could have access to, like my gun and smudged fingerprints that couldn't have been properly processed. After a few hours, one of the judges of the all-white board asked me if I wanted to address the court if I had anything to say before the final verdict. This was the moment I had anticipated since the night I was released from jail. This was what I had prepared for, and I was ready to finally say the things that I've wanted to say my entire life. I stood to my feet, buttoned my suit jacket, and asked if it was okay to stand in the middle of the courtroom so that I could address everyone.

"Today, I stand before each of you under such horrible circumstances. I stand before each of you as a black man who has been accused of committing a crime that does not fit in anything relative to my background, family life, or any of what I have accomplished in my 30 Years of living. While this was one of the hardest experiences of my life, it will never be harder than being a black man in America. I understand that the expectation was for me to stand before you and likely apologize for what I am being accused of, but today I cannot do that. I am not guilty of the crime that you all are trying me for. I am not guilty of the crime that the world has placed on my skin color or my appearance. Just because I'm a black man who grew up in a bad community and ran when I heard gunshots does not make me guilty. Instead, it makes me afraid. It shows that the world has been so negative towards black men that I have to run and be afraid when I am also an officer of the law. I have to be afraid for my own life for the sake of my mother, for the sake of my father, for the sake of my friends and family, and also for the sake of every black man who has walked these streets. Those who had matriculated through life, whether they were able to grow up or were killed before they had the opportunity, I have to be afraid for the sake of everyone.

My only hope that night was to go for a walk after being told that my mother was in her last months of living. The woman who has sacrificed her entire life for my well-being, the person I work so hard to provide something better for when it's not even my responsibility, the same woman who sacrificed everything she loved to take care of everyone else but herself. She is the same woman that told her only son that these were her last days, even while fighting to maintain during a global pandemic. And even in those last days, my mom is sitting right there next to me, fighting alongside me because she knows that this is something that I would never do.

I have always been a person who has held myself to a higher standard. I have influenced that same standard among my friends and other black men in my community. Today I am standing with the same mothers and family members of black men and women whose lives have been taken at the hands of police. The same people who were sworn in to protect and serve the community are the same people we are afraid of. I thought that becoming a police force member would make a difference because I know what was instilled in me from my own parents. I know what it's like to grow up in the hood and not have any opportunities. I know what it's like to look beyond my neighborhood to see Capitol Hill, where all of the white citizens are progressing and making money and doing things that are much bigger than anything anyone in my neighborhood has seen. But, still, I am here on the opposite side of the same law that swore to protect me not just as a black man, not just as an officer, but as a human being. I am on the other side of this thing fighting for my life to prove my innocence towards something that I did not do.

I say to each of you today, no matter how this thing turns out, no matter how hard the circumstances may be, no matter what the verdict turns out to be, I am proud to be black, I am proud to wear my badge, and I am even more proud to see the families of black men and women who have suffered and taken great loss over the last few years, because of police officers who are afraid of black skin, because of white citizens who are afraid of blacks, because of people having a disregard for my black skin, stand with me during this trial. So, yes, I'm on trial for my life. I am on trial, and my life is at your mercy, but I will never stop believing, hoping, praying, and spreading love with hope that there will be a change in our community, that there will be change here in Austin, Texas, that there will be a change in America. And not just change for the sake of African American people, but the diminishing of injustice, in the justice system, against people of color in totality. In recent news, a group of Asian Americans was targeted for no apparent reason, and we're brutally killed. There is a bigger issue in this country that we continue to neglect. In fact, the more hatred and disregard for human life that is spread will continue throughout the nation. So today, your honors, I'm not standing here before you pleading for mercy on my own life. I stand before you pleading for Mercy against every person in this country who has been wrongfully targeted, wrongfully convicted, brutally beaten, slain, and killed without any opportunity to defend themselves, to defend what happened, or even to have a fair trial.

It appears to me that the system doesn't even want people that look Like me to have a fair opportunity to stand before you and fight for our lives. I want to apologize because whatever happened six nights ago, whatever happened that caused my captain, my Superior, someone that I truly admired before all of this, the reason that I fought so hard to improve and be better for better opportunities, whatever caused his life to be taken, whoever framed me for something so harmful and hurtful to our department and to our community, I pray that they are given a fair opportunity for trial, and to explain why they would commit such a heinous crime. But what I won't do, what I won’t stand before you and say, is that I'm guilty. Before I take my seat, as I know I've been before you much too long, I want each of you in this courtroom to look at the families that are sitting to the right and left of me. Look at the families who are still mourning the loss of their loved ones. Look at the families who have been dragged through the media with questions and seeing images of their family members painted in such a horrible light. Look at these families and take note of the accountability this system has lacked for so long. As I said before, I'm not just standing here pleading for my own life; I'm standing here for Sandra Bland for Eric Garner for Ahmaud Aubery for Jonathan Price for Dante Wright, Brianna Taylor, and many others who have been killed by people who simply hate our black skin.

After what I felt was the most compelling speech I'd ever given, I took my seat next to my dad. To my surprise, I was no longer nervous, I no longer felt afraid, and honestly felt that I had done my community a service. I had stood before nine Caucasian judges and told the brutal reality about what was happening right here in our city. I had shared my pain not only as an officer of the law, but as a black man who would never be able to be seen as an equal. No matter how much the department supported my vision for the career, they would always single me out. Just like now, I would always be an outsider because of my skin. Yes, they swore to protect me as equally as the people we serve daily, but deep down, I would always be alienated.

The jury got up from their seats and disappeared behind the tall wood door to the right of them. Slightly nervous, I began bouncing my legs underneath the table and rubbing my hands together repeatedly. My father, Edwards, reached over, placed his hand on my knee and gave a reassuring look. After about an hour, one of the members of the jury, peeped their head in, spoke to the sheriff, and the sheriff walked over and spoke with the judge to the far right. That judge leaned over and shared the message with the next judge and so on. I thought back to when I was in Ms. Biggs classroom. She would lean over, whisper a message in one student's ear, and we'd have to keep the chain going until it got back to her. The message was never the same when it got to her. This was the one moment in that courtroom I felt that my life was no longer mine, but truly in the hands of people who didn't look like me. I witnessed on tv and the media all the time how predominantly white audiences would never show mercy on black people. The slip ups in saying "nigger," their openly racist accidental banter, them literally getting away with murder, yet people of color would be convicted without even getting a fair trial.

One final time, a member of the jury came back into the court room, whispered to the sheriff, and the chain began again. "Dad, what's taking so long?" In that moment, I saw a change in my father's appearance that I hadn't seen the entire time. I saw the tension release from his shoulders as he leaned over to me and said, "Son, sometimes the jury debate about their position on the case. When one person disagrees, it forces them to have to revisit the entire case over again so that they can all come to an agreement. Hopefully it will be over soon." With his briefcase open, I watched my father, my lawyer, place his hand on a small bible and close his eyes for a moment. I looked back at my mother, then around the courtroom at all the people who showed up for me. There was dead silence, and I could literally hear one of the judges breathing heavy through their microphone.

THE FINAL VERDICT

Which Fate will you choose?

Fate One
Fate Two

FATE ONE

THE FIRST DRAW

After about another thirty minutes the jury came back to their seats and stood before the court. The one toward the end, near the judges, handed a sheet of paper to the sheriff and the sheriff handed it to one of the judges on the end. Then, each judge handed the paper to the other to review the final verdict. Once the final judge had read and given approval to the others, they asked everyone in the courtroom for their attention for the final verdict. My father looked at me and I could see the fear in his eyes. My mother was sniffling behind me. It brought pain to me, to hear my mom whispering prayers and crying all the same. Not before long, one of the judges said, "In the case against Korbin D. King vs. Police Captain David R. Grisham, how do you find the defendant? The jury foreperson said, "Your honors, we the jury find the defendant Korbin Dewayne King, guilty of murder in the first degree. The judge replied, "So say you all?" "Yes, your honor," the jury replied in unison.

. . .

THE ENTIRE COURTROOM was in an uproar. My mother yelled out crying and screaming "not my son." I could see all the mothers and families in the courtroom, shaking their heads, crying, and getting up from their seats as if the verdict was too much to bear. "When will it stop?" I heard someone yell out. Immediately my father grabbed me, hugged me tight and said... The fight isn't over

TODAY, I witnessed something firsthand that I can and will never forget. Yes, I was wrongfully convicted of a crime I didn't commit. I recognize that no matter how much we fight as black people, there is never justice for us. There is never an opportunity for us to truly get justice. But more importantly, I witnessed the abundance of love and support my community brought in my honor. I pray that eventually, justice will prevail for all of us!

FATE TWO

NOT EVERY STORY HAS AN ENDING

After about another thirty minutes the jury came back to their seats and stood before the court. The one toward the end, near the judges, handed a sheet of paper to the sheriff and the sheriff handed it to one of the judges on the end. Then, each judge handed the paper to the other to review the final verdict. Once the final judge had read and given approval to the others, they asked everyone in the courtroom for their attention for the final verdict. My father looked at me and I could see the fear in his eyes. My mother was sniffling behind me. It brought pain to me, to hear my mom whispering prayers and crying all the same. Not before long, one of the judges said, "In the case against Korbin D. King vs. Police Captain David R. Grisham, how do you find the defendant? The jury foreperson said, "Your honors, we the jury find the defendant Korbin Dewayne King, not guilty! The judge replied, "So say you all?" "Yes, your honor," the jury replied in unison.

The entire courtroom cheered. My mother yelled out crying and screaming "thank you Jesus." I could see all the mothers and families in the courtroom, crying and being thankful that for once, something good had happened in a case of the sort. My father grabbed me and hugged me, and I returned it, grateful to be able to work toward having a future with both of my parents.

TODAY, I witnessed a small change in my life. While there was a slight change in justice this time around, not much had truly changed. There was still someone who killed my captain. I would likely never be able to have my job back. I will likely never pursue my longtime dream in cyber security. So many people have still taken loses and not seen justice for the things they have witnessed or experienced, but today... my freedom is more than enough to start a journey toward demonstrating the power my people can bring.

UNTIL NEXT TIME...

ABOUT THE AUTHOR

Takara James specializes in Creative Writing. With a bachelor's in English and master's in English and Creative Writing, she helps business savvy and academic driven individuals obtain success through writing. With such passion in the writing industry, Takara launched her online writing firm, Writluxe, which aids in publication, professional writing, and stationery design, bridging the gap between creative development and writing. She initially began her firm writing resumes and from there, her business, Writluxe (written luxury) grew tremendously.

Takara's objective is to continue to be the resource for writers, entrepreneurs, and professionals who wish to grow in their careers, academically, and professionally. As an author of 10 publications, she has the first-hand experience in how to propel oneself toward their destiny. She also holds the following memberships and certifications:

Sigma Tau Delta International English Honors
Modern Language Association, Graduate Class member
The National Society of Leadership and Success
International Association of Professional Writers and Editors
Southern New Hampshire University Creative Writing Review Panel Member

Subscribe to my e-list for more crime fiction books.
Website: www.tmjamesbooks.org
More about Writluxe Writing Firm - www.writluxe.org

facebook.com/tmjamesbooks
twitter.com/tmjamesbooks
instagram.com/tmjamesbooks
amazon.com/Takara-James/e/B07PWG3NFH/ref=ntt_dp_epwbk_0
goodreads.com/authortakarajames
linkedin.com/in/takaramjames

www.ingramcontent.com/pod-product-compliance
Lightning Source LLC
LaVergne TN
LVHW022321200926
848481LV00004B/1387
* 9 7 8 1 7 3 5 9 7 0 1 4 1 *